# THE HOME FRONT
## in the Vietnam War

### WILLIAM THOMAS

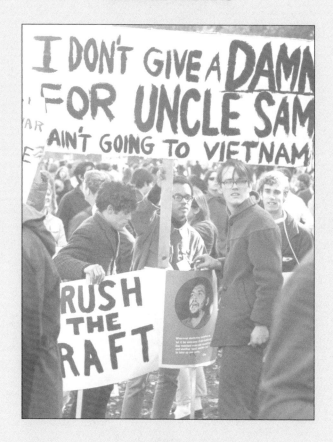

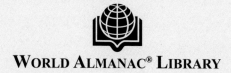

**WORLD ALMANAC® LIBRARY**

Please visit our web site at: www.worldalmanaclibrary.com
For a free color catalog describing World Almanac® Library's list of high-quality books
and multimedia programs, call 1-800-848-2928 (USA) or 1-800-387-3178 (Canada).
World Almanac® Library's fax: (414) 332-3567.

Library of Congress Cataloging-in-Publication Data

Thomas, William, 1947-
    The home front in the Vietnam War / by William Thomas.
        p. cm. — (The American experience in Vietnam)
    Includes bibliographical references and index.
    ISBN 0-8368-5775-5 (lib. bdg.)
    ISBN 0-8368-5782-8 (softcover)
    1. Vietnamese Conflict, 1961-1975—United States—Juvenile literature.  2. United
States—Politics and government—1963-1969—Juvenile literature.  3. United States—
Politics and government—1969-1974—Juvenile literature.  I. Title.  II. Series.
DS558.T45    2005
959.704'31—dc22                                          2004058086

First published in 2005 by
**World Almanac® Library**
330 West Olive Street, Suite 100
Milwaukee, WI  53212  USA

Copyright © 2005 by World Almanac® Library.

Developed by Amber Books Ltd.
Editor: James Bennett
Designer: Colin Hawes
Photo research: Natasha Jones
World Almanac® Library editors: Mark Sachner and Alan Wachtel
World Almanac® Library art direction: Tammy West
World Almanac® Library production: Jessica Morris

Picture Acknowledgements
Cody Images (www.codyimages.com): cover (top left), 11, 12, 28, 40; Corbis: cover (main),
1, 4, 5, 6, 8, 10, 16, 17, 18, 19, 20, 24, 25, 27, 29, 30, 33, 34, 35, 37, 38, 41, 43, 45;
Getty Images: 15, 32; U.S. National Archives: 9.

Printed in Canada

1 2 3 4 5 6 7 8 9 09 08 07 06 05

## About the Author

**WILLIAM THOMAS** is a schoolteacher who lives in Rochester, New York.
He is a returned Peace Corps Volunteer and holds graduate degrees from
Rochester Institute of Technology and Nazareth College. In his career, he has
written materials for children, software documentation, advertising copy,
magazine articles, and training programs.

# Table of Contents

Words that appear in the glossary are printed in **boldface** type
the first time they occur in the text

# Introduction

The Vietnam War (1954–1975) was part of a larger conflict known as the Second Indochina War, which raged in Southeast Asia and involved the nations of Cambodia, Laos, and Vietnam. From 1946 until 1954, the Vietnamese had fought for independence from France during the First Indochina War. When the French were defeated, the country was divided into North and South Vietnam. Vietnamese **communists** controlled North Vietnam and wanted to unify Vietnam under communist rule. Non-communist Vietnamese controlled the South. In the 1950s, the United States and the Soviet Union were in the early years of their struggle over political, economic, and military influence in various parts of the world. Known as the Cold War, this struggle did not pit each nation against the other directly. Rather, each supported other countries that were squared off against one another. In the mid-1950s, the U.S. began training South Vietnam's army, while the Soviet Union and China backed communist North Vietnam. By the mid-1960s, U.S. forces fought alongside the Army of the Republic of Vietnam (ARVN) against the North Vietnamese Army (NVA) and the National Front for the Liberation of Vietnam (NLF).

Initially, most Americans supported the war, especially when U.S. generals and politicians kept saying that it was almost over. As the war continued, however, many Americans began to ask some hard questions. Why couldn't the most powerful nation on Earth defeat some bare-footed **guerrillas**? Why was the United States fighting another country's civil war when U.S. citizens themselves needed help? These questions divided the nation. Many felt that the fight against communism was right and patriotic and respected the decisions of the president and his military **advisors**. Slogans such as "My country, right or wrong!" and "America: love it or leave it!" reflected this position. Others felt the war was unjustified and had no clear aim. They had their slogans, too. Among the favorite chants directed against President Lyndon B. Johnson was: "Hey, hey, L.B.J.! How many kids did you kill today?"

The Vietnam War was the longest war the United States ever fought, and it was the only war it ever lost. The country, however, lost more than just the war. The United States lost faith in its armed forces. U.S. aircraft and tanks weren't effective against an enemy who hid in the jungles, and some U.S. soldiers committed terrible crimes in Vietnam. Many Americans also lost faith in their government when they learned that the country's leaders had lied about how, where, and why the United States was fighting.

As the war dragged on, and more and more dead U.S. **GIs** were sent home in body bags, demonstrations against the U.S. presence in Vietnam grew. National Guard units clashed with college students on campuses across the nation—sometimes with deadly results—and veterans returning home from Vietnam often found themselves the targets of scorn and ridicule.

In 1982, the Vietnam Veterans Memorial was dedicated in Washington, D.C., to commemorate the personnel who died or were declared missing in action in Vietnam. Today, the Vietnam Veterans Memorial serves as a stark reminder of the sacrifice made by the men and women who fought in this unique war.

**Below:** Opposition to the war was not confined to students. Here, delegates at the 1968 Democratic National Convention in Chicago protest U.S. policy on the Vietnam War.

# CHAPTER 1: Stopping Communism

# The Background

**Right:** Communist revolutionary leader Ho Chi Minh led North Vietnam to independence from French colonial rule.

Most Americans strongly supported the United States' early involvement in Vietnam. In their view, the country was helping a small, newly independent nation protect itself from communists. Military officers, government officials, and citizens who were opposed to communism were strongest in support of U.S. actions. As years went by, however, and the war dragged on with no clear hope of victory, even some of the "hawks" began to wonder how the U.S. had gotten into such a mess.

## HOW IT ALL BEGAN

Vietnam was originally a colony of France. During World War II (1939–1945), Japan invaded Vietnam. With the defeat of Japan in 1945, a communist leader named Ho Chi Minh declared Vietnam an independent nation. France wanted to keep its colony and sent an army to fight for it. Using guerrilla tactics similar to those used a decade later against U.S. troops, Ho Chi Minh's Viet Minh independence movement defeated the French in 1954. At a conference in Geneva, Switzerland, to discuss a settlement for the region, Vietnam was divided into two nations, the communist North, led by Ho Chi Minh, and the U.S.-supported South. A condition of the Geneva Accords was that elections would soon be held to reunify Vietnam under a democratically agreed-upon government, but the elections did not take place. In 1955, Ngo Dinh Diem declared himself president of the South. Fighting soon broke out between the two nations due to political and economic differences.

U.S. president Dwight D. Eisenhower sent money and military supplies to the South Vietnamese government, as well as a small group of U.S. troops, referred to as "military advisors," to train its army. China and the Soviet Union sent weapons to North Vietnam. When John F. Kennedy became president in 1960, he increased the number of "advisors" in South Vietnam. These

## FRENCH DEFEAT AT DIEN BIEN PHU

**Above:** Guarded by communist Viet Minh troops, French prisoners of war are marched away after their defeat at Dien Bien Phu.

In 1954, French troops were fighting the communist Viet Minh for control of Vietnam. The French built up a stronghold near a village called Dien Bien Phu. The Viet Minh surrounded it. They took apart field guns and other large weapons, used thousands of men to carry the parts up the high hills around the French position, and then reassembled the weapons and attacked. Dien Bien Phu's airstrip closed down. Airplanes dropped food and ammunition by parachute, but the Viet Minh captured many of the supplies. Closed off from the outside world and under constant fire, the French forces surrendered. Soon after, Vietnam was officially divided into two countries, the communist North and noncommunist South.

"advisors" were supposed to be training the Vietnamese, not actually fighting. Yet, U.S. pilots were flying bombing missions, and U.S. soldiers were accompanying South Vietnamese forces into combat. In a press conference in January 1962, Kennedy denied that U.S. troops were engaged in combat in Vietnam. This assertion was one of the earliest false statements about the war made to the U.S. public. It was not the last.

By the end of 1962, the number of U.S. military "advisors" in Vietnam had grown from 700 to 12,000, and the South Vietnamese army continued to lose ground to the communists. Furthermore, President Diem's government was losing the support of the Vietnamese people. On November 1, 1963, a group of generals took over the government. Diem fled but was captured and shot dead. Three weeks later, President Kennedy was assassinated and Lyndon B. Johnson became U.S. president. Things continued to go badly for the South Vietnamese government and its army. The generals who overthrew President Diem were themselves overthrown. Communist guerrilla fighters, known as the Viet Cong, forced the South Vietnamese armed forces out of the countryside and into the towns and cities.

## THE GULF OF TONKIN INCIDENT

On August 2, 1964, the Navy warship USS *Maddox* was on patrol in the Gulf of Tonkin, off the coast of North Vietnam, when it was approached by three North Vietnamese Navy (NVN) torpedo boats. The NVN boats ignored a warning shot, so the *Maddox* opened fire. Fighter planes were also called in from a nearby aircraft carrier. The U. S., claiming it had been fired upon, warned that any further "unprovoked" action would be met by force. On August 4, the *Maddox* returned to patrol the area with another ship, the *C. Turner Joy*. A radar operator on

**Left:** One of a series of controversial photographs released at the time of the Gulf of Tonkin incident, this picture shows a North Vietnamese patrol boat under fire from the USS *Maddox*. U. S. claims that the *Maddox* had been fired upon have been the subject of some debate. What is clear, however, is that the Gulf of Tonkin incident gave President Johnson the argument he needed to persuade Congress to authorize the president to wage war in Vietnam.

## "VIETNAM IS THE PLACE"

**Right:** President Kennedy met with Soviet premier Nikita Khrushchev at a summit conference in Vienna, Austria, in June 1961. The two leaders clashed on several issues, including the situation in Southeast Asia.

In the years following World War II, fear of communism was one of the major forces shaping U.S. foreign policy. Cuba, just 90 miles (145 kilometers) from the U.S. coast, became a communist nation in 1958 after its U.S.-supported government was overthrown in a revolution led by Fidel Castro. In 1962, the Soviet Union tried to base nuclear missiles in Cuba. In East Germany, the Soviet-backed government built the Berlin Wall, dividing that city into free and communist zones. The communist government in China was sending troops into Tibet and Mongolia. Both China and the Soviet Union were sending military supplies and money to the communist government in North Vietnam. The United States saw Vietnam as a place to take a stand against the spread of communism. In 1961, President Kennedy met with the leader of the Soviet Union, Nikita Khrushchev. Afterward Kennedy told a reporter, "Now we have a problem in making our power credible, and Vietnam is the place to do it."

board the *Maddox* detected some suspicious signals on the surface, and both ships opened fire at the mysterious vessels. The United States claimed that the North Vietnamese had fired first — a claim that many disputed then and coninue to dispute. The next day, however, President Johnson appeared on television and said that U.S. ships had been attacked by North Vietnamese forces. Johnson asked Congress to give him the authority to "take all necessary measures" to protect U.S. forces from attacks. On August 10, 1964, Congress passed a bill called the Gulf of Tonkin Resolution that gave the president power to wage war in Vietnam. Polls found that 85 percent of Americans supported the resolution. Almost no one knew it may have been based on a lie.

By the end of 1964, 267 Americans had been killed in Vietnam, even though all the U.S. troops in Vietnam were still considered advisors. But in March 1965, when President Johnson sent another 3,500 Marines to Vietnam, they did not pretend to be advisors. Their mission was to search out and destroy the enemy.

**Below:** In December 1964, Viet Cong guerrillas in Saigon set off a car bomb that killed two Americans.

# Against the War

**Right:** An antiwar march takes place in Washington, D.C., on January 19, 1969, the day before the inauguration of Richard Nixon as president.

In 1965, President Johnson's policies still had strong public support. By 1967, however, that began to change. Protests were sporadic at first; then there were more and more of them. People opposed the sending of U.S. troops to fight on the other side of the world; they opposed the huge financial cost of the war; they felt they had been misled by their government; and they were horrified by the number of young men who were being killed. Eventually, antiwar demonstrations became the largest of any staged over any issue in U.S. history.

## COUNTERCULTURE AND THE GENERATION GAP

By the mid 1960s, a growing generation gap existed in the United States. Beginning with rock 'n' roll and Elvis Presley in the 1950s and continuing with "British Invasion" bands such as the Beatles and the Rolling Stones, American youth culture began to look and sound different from the culture of the previous generation. The Vietnam War and the protests against it were the spark for many young people to turn against almost everything in mainstream American society. As the 1960s progressed, many of these "hippies" showed their rebellion by wearing wild fashions, such as tie-dyed shirts and long hair; listening to protest music by artists such as Bob Dylan and Joan Baez; experimenting with marijuana and other drugs; and protesting against the war.

## PORTRAIT OF A PROTESTER: LISA KALVELAGE

Lisa Kalvelage was a mother and housewife in San Diego, California. In May 1966, she and some other women were arrested when they tried to prevent **napalm** from being loaded onto a ship bound for Vietnam. When asked why she did it, Kalvelage said she grew up in Germany during World War II. After marrying an American soldier and moving to the United States, people always asked if her parents had resisted Hitler and the terrible crimes he committed. Kalvelage didn't know. In years to come, she said, she wanted her six children to know that their mother had tried to prevent crimes in Vietnam.

Many hippies thought of their antiwar activities as part of a radical, more peaceful "counterculture" movement against the "establishment"—the mainstream American culture that sent U.S. soldiers to fight in Vietnam. These protests did not sit well with some Americans, many of them older people who believed that young people were attacking basic American values and culture. The disapproval of their elders did not bother the hippies, who expressed their counterculture attitude with slogans like, "Don't trust anyone over thirty."

Especially in its early days, the antiwar movement held a close relationship with the Civil Rights movement. In many parts of the United States, the South especially, African Americans could not live in the same neighborhoods, attend the same schools, or eat at the same restaurants as whites. In some places, they were even prevented from voting. Leaders in both movements believed that the Vietnam War was taking money and attention away from the problems of African Americans. One protester asked, "What kind of America is it whose response to poverty and oppression in South Vietnam is napalm and **defoliation**, but whose response to poverty and oppression in Mississippi is silence?" Martin Luther King, Jr. often spoke out against the war. In 1967, he led an antiwar march in New York City that drew 100,000 people.

## DRAFT RESISTANCE

The issue that most clearly showed differences between war supporters and war opponents was the draft. Officially known as the Selective Service, the draft forced men to serve in the military or go to jail. Even so, many young men refused. Some young men mailed their draft cards back to the government as a sign of resistance. Others publicly burned their cards, an act that carried a five-year prison sentence. At rallies, young men chanting, "Hell no, we won't go!" and posters declaring that, "Girls say yes to guys who say no" spoke volumes about how many young people felt about the draft. At many colleges, students tried to prevent military recruiters from visiting their campuses. Some young men went so far as to leave the country to avoid the draft, going to Sweden or Canada. Near the U.S./Canadian border, people who opposed the war set up an underground railroad to help draft resisters. A group in Toronto published a small book called *Manual for Draft-Age Immigrants to Canada*. It was sold in college bookstores across the U.S. According to one estimate, almost 100,000 young men resisted the draft by going to prison, leaving the U.S., or deserting after being drafted into the army.

**Above:** Members of the New York City Transportation Union display their support for U.S. forces with flags and signs in a 1967 pro-Vietnam War demonstration.

## WIDE-RANGING PROTESTS

Opinion polls in 1966 showed that President Johnson had lost much of his earlier popularity, largely due to the antiwar movement. In 1967, Johnson sought to regain his approval rating with a public relations campaign in which several military and political figures promised the nation that victory was in sight. Massive attacks by the North Vietnamese and Viet Cong in January 1968, known as the Tet Offensive, foiled Johnson's campaign, however, by showing that the situation in Vietnam was still extremely volatile. Shortly afterward, General William Westmoreland, who was in charge of the U.S. military in Vietnam, asked for 206,000 additional troops. Many people in the United States questioned the need for these troops if victory was in sight. The announcement caused a wave of protests and unrest.

## THE DRAFT

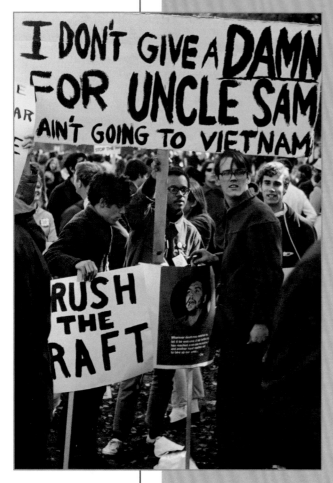

**Above:** Young men protest against the draft and the war at a 1967 rally in Washington, D.C.

During the Vietnam War, men who were drafted had to serve in the military for two years. Failure to obey could mean a prison sentence of up to ten years. At first, the draft board in each town could decide who to call. In December 1969, the draft was changed to a nationwide lottery system based on birthdays. The days of the year were drawn from a basket one at a time; men born on the first date drawn were drafted first, while those born on dates picked later were drafted later. Men were excused from the draft if they were married or medically unfit. **Conscientious objectors** were also excused. These were people who were able to demonstrate that they should not serve in the armed forces for moral or religious reasons. Notable among these was boxer Muhammad Ali, who said his faith as a Black Muslim forbade him to kill. Men could also receive a deferment—to postpone draft eligibility—if they were in college full time. Many people were concerned about the fairness of the draft, because it was most often the poor or those without connections who were drafted.

Although draft resisters and college students got most of the attention, they weren't the only people protesting against the war. Religious and civil rights groups demonstrated against it, too. Mothers Against the Vietnam War became a nationwide organization, reflecting the fact that the American people were becoming unwilling to support a war in Asia with the lives of their sons. Influential figures, including the boxer Muhammad Ali and the actress Jane Fonda, added their voices to the growing chorus of protest.

In 1967, a group of hippies marched to the Pentagon and put daisies in the rifle barrels of the military police. They were tear-gassed but the term "flower power" had taken on new vigor. Benjamin Spock, an elderly doctor who had written several famous books on baby care, was arrested twice for antiwar activities. In response, war supporters held rallies and burned his books.

By March 1968, President Johnson was disillusioned and tired. Partly because of the strength of public opposition to the war, and partly because he felt that his presence would have undermined any future negotiations with North Vietnam to end the war, he decided not to seek another term of office.

## MY LAI AND CAMBODIA

Events in Southeast Asia continued to increase opposition to the war. In 1969, a horrifying story reached the U.S. public. In a small Vietnamese village called My Lai, U.S. soldiers killed more than 300 unarmed men, women, and children. The news was kept secret for months, but when the story of the My Lai massacre was revealed, even those who supported the war were shocked.

Thousands of protesters took to the streets across the country, and a massive demonstration took place in Washington, D.C. Soon afterward, newly elected president Richard Nixon announced that he would begin to withdraw U.S. troops from

## PORTRAIT OF A PROTESTER: TOM HAYDEN

Tom Hayden was a founding member of a nationwide group called Students for a Democratic Society. In the early 1960s, he was active in civil rights work in the South and in the North. He later shifted his attention to the Vietnam War. Hayden was arrested in Chicago during the 1968 Democratic Convention. He and six others were charged with conspiracy to incite riots. The arrested protesters became known as the Chicago Seven. They were all found guilty, but the convictions were overturned. Hayden married actress Jane Fonda, who also was an outspoken opponent of the war. Years later, he was elected to the California State Senate. Hayden served for many years, supporting environmental issues and the rights of women and minorities.

Vietnam. Protest activity slowed down across the nation, but the calm did not last long.

North Vietnam was sending soldiers and supplies to the Viet Cong through the jungles of neighboring Cambodia, a country that had declared itself neutral in the U.S.–Vietnam war. In March 1969, Nixon ordered U.S. aircraft to begin bombing border areas in Cambodia. These attacks were kept secret from Congress and even from many military leaders. On April 30, 1970, Nixon appeared on television to announce that U.S. troops were staging a land invasion of Cambodia.

In the next few days, parts of the United States were engulfed in the most serious protest incidents since 1968. Many believed

## NIXON AND THE BOMBING OF CAMBODIA

In the summer of 1969, the *New York Times* exposed the secret bombing of Cambodia and began to publish secret Defense Department documents on Vietnam. When the secret bombing campaign was revealed, members of Congress were outraged. Many believed that the president had violated the United States Constitution. To many members of the public, it seemed that Nixon was secretly widening the war even while he promised he was ending it. Once again, protests swept across the nation.

**Left:** President Richard Nixon explaining his Cambodia policy in a television broadcast in April 1970.

that Nixon had broken his campaign promise not to escalate the war. Protest was strongest, however, among college protesters, who Nixon referred to as "bums, you know, blowing up the campuses." On May 4, soldiers in the Ohio National Guard shot seventeen students on the campus of Kent State University, killing four. Within days, student protests shut down more than

400 colleges and universities, and more than 100,000 citizens marched in an antiwar demonstration in Washington, D.C.

## "THE LAST MAN TO DIE"

A new group joined the protesters: Vietnam Veterans Against the War. In April 1971, more than 1,000 veterans set up a tent camp in Washington, D.C., to protest the war. Some were in wheelchairs; some were missing arms or legs; many had scars from wounds received in Vietnam. Police put up a fence to keep the veterans away from the Capitol building. Hundreds of them tossed their combat medals over the fence. One of the veterans asked a Senate committee, "How do you ask a man to be the last man to die in Vietnam? How do you ask a man to be the last man to die for a mistake?" It was two more years before the last American soldier died in combat in Vietnam. Protests against the war continued until then.

**Right:** Vietnam veterans joined students and other groups in antiwar protests such as this one in Raleigh, North Carolina, in 1972.

## KENT STATE

On May 1 and 2, 1970, students at Kent State University in Ohio held rallies after President Nixon announced the invasion of Cambodia. Despite the fact that Kent State had no history of violent demonstrations against the war, the protests escalated, and on the evening of May 2, someone set fire to an old wooden building on campus that was used for Reserve Officer Training Corps (ROTC) classes. These classes prepared college students to become military officers and were often targets for student protests. The governor of Ohio was outraged and ordered National Guard troops to the campus. On May 4, after a day of tension as the Guardsmen occupied the university, more than 1,500 students gathered to watch the Guardsmen, and some yelled insults at them. When the nervous soldiers fired tear gas canisters, students picked them up and threw them back. Clouds of gas and smoke filled the air. An officer pointed at the students, and the Guardsmen opened fire with their rifles. When the gunfire ended, four students lay dead; thirteen more were wounded. Two of those killed had simply been walking between buildings to change classes. A trial later acquitted the Guardsmen of any crime. To this day, exactly why the Guardsmen opened fire is unknown.

**Above:** A young woman reacts to the sight of the body of a student shot dead by National Guard troops at Kent State University on May 4, 1970.

# The Media

**Right:** Vietnamese soldiers, civilian photographers, and journalists observe the aftermath of a misdirected napalm attack on a village near Trang Bang in South Vietnam. The attack killed at least four children and one woman.

The war that was fought in the jungles, rice paddies, and cities of Vietnam was replayed each night in living rooms across the United States. It has been said that the media—newspapers, news magazines, and especially television—played a greater role in Vietnam than in any U.S. war before or since. Journalists sent home stories and close-up pictures of soldiers fighting and dying. Americans saw Vietnamese women and children running from burning villages. Perhaps most significant of all, the United States watched hundreds and hundreds of flag-covered coffins roll off military aircraft as the dead were brought home.

## THE POWER OF THE PRESS

There were two reasons why Americans saw these powerful images, and saw them quickly. The first was technology. Early fax and **teletype** machines, plus regular jet airline services, made it possible to transmit stories and film from Vietnam to the United States within hours. This was impossible during World War II or the Korean War (1950–1953). The second reason was government policy—or the lack of it. In Vietnam, reporters and photographers had almost unlimited access to the war. In contrast to today's "embedded" war reporters, who are restricted in what they can report and are accompanied by military liaison officers at all times, reporters in Vietnam could act entirely independently. Taking huge risks, they flew on helicopter missions, marched into the jungle with the infantry, and walked behind tanks during major battles. They could go practically anywhere their courage and strength would take them—and they could broadcast what they liked.

The Vietnam War caused a division in U.S. society, and the media reported on it often. Some military and political leaders believed the media caused the division, but most experts say that wasn't true. When the Vietnam War began, the overwhelming

## INTO BATTLE WITH A CAMERA

Reporters and photographers in Vietnam were in the villages, in the Army camps, and on board the helicopters. It was a dangerous job, and more than sixty journalists were killed while doing it. Many of them were friends of George Esper, who spent eleven years covering the war as a reporter for the Associated Press. He said, "War propelled them into harm's way with the only weapons they ever knew: their cameras." According to Esper, the government often attempted to paint a rosy picture of military actions in Vietnam. When journalists' stories said otherwise, the government blamed the press for turning the public against the war. According to Esper, however, "We were just telling the public what we saw. We were more honest with the American people than their own government was."

**Right:** Television coverage of actual combat was broadcast regularly on U.S. television. Here, a CBS camera crew interviews U.S. troops in 1967. TV channels competed for dramatic news footage, so explosions and fire were much more likely to be seen on TVs in the U.S. than more peaceful scenes.

majority of U.S. newspapers and news magazines supported it. The media continued to report favorably on the war throughout most of the early 1960s. In those years, journalists almost never questioned why the United States was in Vietnam or said that the troops should leave. This pattern changed, however, not because of the media, but because of events such as My Lai, the secret bombing of Cambodia, and the Tet Offensive, that the media needed to report.

## DISTRUST

In 1964, *Time* magazine ran a story about the attacks on U.S. ships in the Gulf of Tonkin. The story gave specific details about the number of enemy vessels, their movements, and the types of guns they used. This information was given to the magazine by U.S. government officials and military officers, so *Time* assumed it was true. It wasn't. In February 1968, Senator James W. Fulbright set up an investigation into the incident, which found that the U.S. government had misled Congress—and the American people—over the incident.

When the United States began bombing North Vietnam, the Johnson administration said that the United States was attacking only military targets: bridges, factories, and missile sites. In 1966, however, *New York Times* reporter Harrison Salisbury became the first U.S. journalist actually to visit North Vietnam. Salisbury reported that homes, offices, schools, and hospitals were being destroyed. Although it is certainly true that in a guerrilla war it is hard to distinguish between military and civilian targets, journalists soon began to distrust everything the government and the military told them. This was especially true in South Vietnam. Late each afternoon, military officers in Saigon (the capital city of South Vietnam during the war) gave a **briefing** for reporters, telling them all of the day's events. Newspeople, who were free to check the facts with soldiers, civilians, and their own eyes, found the information so unreliable that they began calling the briefings "The Five O'Clock Follies."

## 1968: A TERRIBLE YEAR

Although supporters of the war often said that television news and programming turned people against the war, a *Newsweek* magazine poll taken in 1967 showed that most Americans thought television reporting helped them support the war. Soon after that poll, President Johnson told the country that U.S. policies were succeeding, that the war was under control, and that its end was in sight. He was wrong. The months that followed Johnson's "the end is in sight" report were the most terrible of the war, both in Vietnam and on the home front. The media captured events for all of the United States to see:

- In January 1968, the North Vietnamese and Viet Cong staged a massive assault, known as the Tet Offensive, against towns and cities all over the South. Even the U.S. embassy in Saigon was attacked.

## THE TET OFFENSIVE

Throughout most of the war, the Viet Cong and their North Vietnamese allies fought mainly in the jungles and countryside. In January 1968, there was a dramatic change in that strategy. The Tet Offensive was a coordinated series of fierce attacks on more than one hundred targets in Vietnam's largest cities and towns. This onslaught surprised President Johnson and his commanding generals, who had said that the enemy could not mount such major attacks and had assured the American people that victory and peace were near. Media reporting of the event helped persuade many members of the public that Johnson had been misleading them about the war. The Tet Offensive was a major setback to both the war effort and to U.S. credibility. It also prompted a tired and defeated Johnson to announce that he would not seek another term of office. By the middle of 1968, most Americans believed that the war could not be won.

**Above:** U.S. Army armored personnel carriers drive through the ruined streets of Saigon. Images like this showing the aftermath of Viet Cong attacks profoundly shocked the U.S. public.

- In February, Saigon's chief of police marched a suspected Viet Cong guerrilla down a street. In broad daylight, he shot the handcuffed man in the head. The murder was shown on television around the world.
- In March, President Johnson announced that he would not seek re-election. War opponents celebrated this as a victory for their

**Above:** Colonel Nguyen Ngoc Loan, chief of the Saigon police, takes "justice" into his own hands and executes a Viet Cong suspect on the street in February 1968. Images like this did much to turn the public against the war.

cause. Many journalists believed that the Tet Offensive killed Johnson's hopes of winning either the war or the election.

● In August, the Democratic National Convention in Chicago was a magnet for the antiwar movement. Every night, television news showed mobs of protesters in the parks and streets, and images of Chicago policemen firing tear gas, clubbing demonstrators, and loading them into vans. Events at the convention dramatically widened the gap between war supporters and opponents.

After 1968, U.S. public opinion began to turn against the war. Richard M. Nixon was elected president with the promise that he would bring the Vietnam War to an end. However, the secret bombing of Cambodia in 1969, and its invasion by U.S. troops in 1970, led to fierce and angry protests. The situation got worse for Nixon in 1971, when a set of secret government documents

## THE MOST TRUSTED MAN IN THE U.S.

Walter Cronkite's deep voice and bushy eyebrows were familiar to nearly everyone in the United States. As anchor of The CBS Evening News, he was known for his fairness and intelligence. He was often called "the most trusted man in the United States." A politician once said that Cronkite's opinion "might well change the vote of thousands of people." Certainly, Cronkite's reports on Vietnam had great impact. Before the 1968 Tet Offensive, Cronkite's views of the war were balanced. After Tet, however, he stopped broadcasting the administration's predictions of winning the war. Instead, Cronkite said he was "more certain than ever that the bloody experience of Vietnam" would not end in a U.S. victory. The majority of the American people believed him.

**Above:** Walter Cronkite anchors the news on CBS television on August 7, 1967.

was leaked to the *New York Times*. Known as the Pentagon Papers, the documents described how the U.S. government had lied about actions in Vietnam, listed mistakes the government had made, and revealed that there was no plan to end the war. By then, even many who believed in the war thought that U.S. policies were failing, as the media began to reveal the truth about Vietnam.

# Returning Vets

**Right:** A disabled Vietnam veteran sits and remembers in the National Cathedral in Washington, D.C.

Soldiers in Vietnam referred to it as "the world." It was home. It was anywhere except "the Nam." But returning veterans faced a range of problems when they returned to the United States. There were no cheers, no parades, few "Welcome Home" signs—except in their parents' windows—just the feeling that they were being received by a nation that seemed less eager to view them with sympathy than with hostility. Equally distressing were the long-term mental and physical effects of the war, with many veterans affected by drug addiction, exposure to toxic chemicals, and recurring nightmares of the horrors of combat.

## A DIFFERENT KIND OF WAR

Combat in Vietnam was different from earlier wars. Author Philip Caputo has noted that Marines who fought in the Pacific during World War II were actually in combat for just six to eight weeks during their entire tour of duty. In Vietnam, troops were in combat nearly all of the time. On patrols, there were always booby traps and land mines, even when soldiers were not actually fighting. Camps could be hit by **mortar** rounds and rockets at any time of the day or night. Furthermore, enemies were often not in uniform, so it was hard to tell them apart from ordinary civilians. It was an environment where there was no relief from the stress of war. As a result, many returning vets suffered from psychological problems. They had nightmares and daytime **flashbacks** to the horrible things they had seen in combat. Doctors called it post traumatic stress syndrome. John Kerry, a decorated veteran who later became a senator and Democratic presidential nominee, told about his return to the U.S. "There I was," he said, "a week out of the jungle, flying from San Francisco to New York. I fell asleep and woke up screaming, probably a nightmare. The other passengers moved away from me—a reaction I noticed more and more in the months ahead."

**Right:** A U.S. C-123 aircraft sprays defoliant, commonly known as Agent Orange, on the dense jungles of South Vietnam in 1970. The program was largely ineffective and caused horrific injuries to those who came into contact with the chemicals.

## AGENT ORANGE

The Viet Cong and North Vietnamese used the dense jungles of their homeland to hide troop movements and supply routes. To counteract this, the United States developed chemicals called defoliants. When sprayed from airplanes, these chemicals killed all the leaves on trees in an area, so that enemy troops could be seen. The defoliant used most often was Agent Orange, so-called because the barrels it came in were marked with orange stripes. Many veterans and Vietnamese civilians who were exposed to Agent Orange came down with lung and nerve diseases, and some developed skin cancer. Their children had high rates of birth defects. For years, the government denied that Agent Orange had caused any of this and refused to treat veterans for these problems.

## THE "GOOD WAR"

Many Vietnam veterans had fathers who had served in World War II. The differences between how these two groups were treated are almost impossible to imagine. Americans often refer to World War II as the "good war" because Japan attacked the United States without warning, and Germany declared war first and posed a concrete threat to the rest of the world. The U.S. people had good reasons to fight, and those on the home front banded together to support the war effort. There were nationwide celebrations when the war ended, and veterans were welcomed home. They were thanked for what they had done; they were asked to speak to schools and Scout troops; they were offered jobs. The men who fought against Germany and Japan were treated as heroes. None of this was true for Vietnam veterans. The Vietnam War had been unpopular and unsuccessful, and some veterans received abuse from those at home who had been strongly against the war.

**Left:** Wives and women in uniform welcome home World War II veterans as their ship pulls into New York City in June 1945. In contrast, returning Vietnam veterans faced scorn and rejection from a changed society.

## DRUGS

Especially during the later years of the war, marijuana, opium, and heroin were available throughout Vietnam. Some was supplied by the Viet Cong as a weapon against the United States and some by South Vietnamese dealers looking to make money. Fear, the stress of guerrilla warfare, and the horrors they saw on the battlefield caused some soldiers to turn to drugs for relief. An official estimate made in 1971 said that almost one-third of

**Right:** This Memorial Day parade was held in New York City in 1985. It was not until years after the war ended that Vietnam veterans received any recognition for their service.

**Left:** The United States was slow to realize that all veterans, even those of unpopular wars, deserved the nation's thanks and respect.

## PORTRAIT OF A VETERAN: DWIGHT "SKIP" JOHNSON

When Dwight "Skip" Johnson's platoon was ambushed, he pulled a wounded soldier from a burning tank; killed several guerrillas with a pistol and rifle, fighting until he ran out of ammunition; and then rescued another injured comrade. For his actions, Johnson received the Medal of Honor. Johnson came home, however, to live in a Detroit slum. He had terrible nightmares. He had stomach problems. He couldn't eat or sleep; he couldn't keep a job. His bills mounted. His house was taken away. Desperate for money, Johnson tried to rob a grocery store. After surviving bullets in Vietnam, he was shot and killed by police in his home town. Johnson was buried in Arlington National Cemetery, and an honor guard fired a salute. A hero was home at last.

## PORTRAIT OF A VETERAN: GARY BEIKIRCH

Gary Beikirch was a medic in the Special Forces, known as the Green Berets. When his camp was attacked, Beikirch repeatedly ran through enemy fire to rescue and treat injured comrades. Although wounded several times himself, Beikirch continued to help others until he collapsed. For his actions, Beikirch received the Medal of Honor. Beikirch's life changed while he was recovering from his wounds in an Army hospital. "I realized I couldn't make it on my own," he said, and he turned to God. After leaving the Army, he studied for the ministry and became a pastor. It took Beikirch years to come to terms with his war experiences. When he did, he became active in veterans' affairs, working at outreach centers and speaking to veterans' groups. Today, Beikirch is a middle-school guidance counselor, still helping others.

returning veterans were addicted to some kind of illegal drug. These veterans needed help to combat these addictions when they came home. Few of them got it.

## REJECTION

As the war became more and more unpopular at home, veterans sometimes became targets for the public's anger and frustration. When veterans looked for jobs or applied to colleges, many felt their military service was held against them. Veterans had done their duty, but many came back with unexplained illnesses, drug addictions, or mental problems. They needed help, but when they came home, they were rejected. Even the government that sent them to Vietnam sometimes rejected the veterans by failing to recognize or treat some of their problems.

Perhaps the worst feeling of all for veterans was that of being unwanted. After America learned of the My Lai massacre, returning veterans were called "baby killers." One soldier who lost an arm in combat was stopped on the street by a young man who pointed to his stump and asked, "Did that happen in Vietnam?" When the veteran said yes, the young man replied, "Serves you right."

## VETERANS' ORGANIZATIONS

**Left:** A speaker addresses a meeting of the Vietnam Veterans of America. The yellow rectangle with three red stripes on his cap is a representation of the South Vietnamese flag.

More than those from any other war, Vietnam veterans needed help when they returned, and many organizations reached out to provide it:

● Veteran's Administration hospitals and clinics across the country provided care and counseling for wounded, sick, or disabled veterans.

● The American Legion and the Veterans of Foreign Wars (VFW) were created after World War I (1914–1918) for men who had served. These organizations welcomed Vietnam veterans, offering them friendship, understanding, and sometimes, financial help.

● The Vietnam Veterans of America (VVA) was formed to assist war veterans, their widows, orphans, and children. The VVA also **lobbied** the government about veterans' issues.

● Across the country, local outreach programs provided "veteran to veteran" aid to those who needed job training, education, help with drug or alcohol problems, or just to talk with someone else who had "been there."

# A Time to Heal

**Right:** A U.S. Marine salutes wooden boxes containing the remains of servicemen listed as missing in action (MIA) before they are loaded aboard a military aircraft in Hanoi in 1994.

On January 29, 1973, the United States, South Vietnam, and North Vietnam signed documents that officially ended the war. The last U.S. soldiers left Vietnam on March 29. On that same day, North Vietnam released 587 U.S. prisoners of war (POWs). Many of them were pilots or aircraft crew members. Some had been in prison for five years or more. All of them had suffered greatly. Air Force planes were sent to Hanoi (the capital of North Vietnam during the war) to fly them home. Unlike most other Vietnam veterans, these men received a hero's welcome. When the planes landed in the United States, some of the returning POWs got down on their knees and kissed the ground. Others rushed to their wives and children. Those families were the lucky ones.

**Above:** Released U.S. prisoners of war (POWs) cheer as their plane leaves North Vietnam in 1973.

## MIA

At the end of the war, there were more than twenty-five hundred Americans listed as missing in action (MIA). They were pilots who were last seen parachuting from damaged aircraft and soldiers who disappeared during heavy combat. They were helicopter crews who never returned to their bases. No one knew if these men were alive or dead, only that they were missing. Many family members and veterans' groups believed that some of those missing were still being held as prisoners. As time passed and tensions eased between the United States and the communist leadership of Vietnam, the two governments began to cooperate. During the Carter, Reagan, and Clinton administrations, the remains of hundreds of soldiers were found,

## A LASTING IMPACT

**Above:** A Vietnam veteran protests the U.S. invasion of Iraq in 2003.

The Vietnam War had a lasting impact on the United States and the legal basis on which it could go to war. The War Powers Resolution limits the president's power to commit troops to action. The president must now get Congressional approval first. The Vietnam War also showed how greatly protests and public opinion, shaped by the media, can influence government policies. In every U.S. military action since then, generals, politicians, journalists, and ordinary citizens have worried about getting involved in "another Vietnam:" a war that the U.S. cannot win without committing vast numbers of troops—and cannot easily withdraw from either without severe political implications.

If the U.S. government learned nothing else from Vietnam, it learned the power of stories and pictures. In both Afghanistan and Iraq, the presence of reporters on the battlefield has been strictly controlled, and at home, President George W. Bush refused to allow photographs or film of soldiers' coffins coming home to be published.

identified, and returned home for burial. Some eighteen hundred are still missing, however, and may never be found.

## THE COST TO VIETNAM

The fighting in Vietnam did not end when the United States left. For two more years, the North and South battled each other. In April 1975, North Vietnamese forces captured Saigon. The United States closed its embassy, and the last Americans left. Vietnam became a united country under a communist government. The war and its aftermath caused many Vietnamese to flee the country, especially those who had served in the South Vietnamese government. Over one million of these people came to the United States. Those who remained in Vietnam, whether North or South, lived in a decimated country. Airports, roads, railways, and factories were destroyed. Napalm and Agent Orange made fields and farms useless for years afterward. Leftover land mines and bombs still kill and injure people today. During the war, more than two million Vietnamese were killed, three million were wounded, and hundreds of thousands of children were orphaned.

**Below:** A Marine Corps veteran in Washington, D.C., displays the Flag of Release, the emblem of the POW/MIA movement in the U.S. The combat boots in the photo represent those still missing.

## THE COST TO THE U.S.

According to one estimate, the total cost of the war was two hundred billion dollars ($200,000,000,000). In human terms, over 58,000 Americans died in Vietnam and 150,000 more were wounded, many of whom lost eyes or limbs or were paralyzed. Thousands more returned from the war racked by illnesses or addicted to drugs. There were social costs for the United States, as well. Although harder to

## VETERANS MEMORIAL

The Vietnam Veterans Memorial is different from all other war monuments in the United States. It was created by two very different people: a wounded veteran and a young woman. Jan Scruggs wanted a memorial for his dead and missing comrades. Many people thought that the war had been so unpopular no one would give money to remember it or its veterans. Scruggs believed in himself, however, and in the United States. In less than two years, he and his friends raised more than eight million dollars. Scruggs then went to Congress to ask for land on which to build the memorial. He got it. Maya Ying Lin was an art student at Yale University. She visited the grassy site chosen for the memorial and thought about how death keeps hurting people, like a wound that never quite heals. She said, "The idea occurred to me there on the site. I had an impulse to cut open the earth. The grass would grow back, but the cut would remain." Her design was chosen from among more than 1,400 entries. As Ying Lin said, the grass has grown back. Inside the cut, carved into two black stone walls, are the names of the 58,235 men and women who died in Vietnam.

measure, they were quite high. Just as the nation had been divided over the war as it was being fought in the 1960s and 1970s, many of those divisions became a feature of U.S. culture, society, and government in the years following the war. To this day, much of what Americans take for granted as attitudes toward government—and the expression of those attitudes in music, literature, film, and popular protests—was shaped by the Vietnam era. During the Vietnam War, many Americans became skeptical about the use of their country's military power. The impact of those doubts can be seen in U.S. policies and actions to this day.

## HEALING THE WOUNDS

President Jimmy Carter took important early steps in healing the United States' war wounds. In 1976, he **pardoned** the young men who had left the country to avoid the draft. This angered many veterans' groups, but Carter thought it was necessary to help bring Americans back together. In 1979, he announced the first Vietnam Veterans Week, saying, "The nation still has a

GERRY L STARK
RICHARD W TOSCHI
DONALD W HART
ARNOLD O NAKKERUD
GEORGE W SCHOOK
LEONARD W ROBERSON
FRANK M BOZZELLO
RONALD J JOHNSON
JOHN T MULLAN
ROBERT E CLOWE
RICHARD G THIBAULT
ARCHIE W MORRIS
J FORREST G TREMBLEY
DAVID K AASEN
RENE L MALARZ
EDWARD J JACOBS
DENNIS W COLE

moral debt to these boys." Land was set aside for the Vietnam Veterans Memorial. President Ronald Reagan continued to press Vietnam to help locate and return the remains of American MIAs. On November 11, 1982, the Vietnam Veterans Memorial was consecrated in Washington, D.C., a simple granite wall inscribed with the names of every American who died in Vietnam. President Bill Clinton began to rebuild relations with Vietnam. He lifted economic restrictions on the country in 1994. In 1995, a U.S. embassy opened in Vietnam.

Some veterans eventually returned to Vietnam. Among them was Gary Beikirch, who went back as part of a group trying to learn about MIAs. It was an emotional trip. For years, Beikirch had kept a hatred for the Viet Cong, but now he knew that he had to forgive. "You have to realize that war was one thing," Beikirch said, "but if you let the hate from the war stay inside you, you're not a whole person."

**Above:** The Vietnam Veterans Memorial in Washington, D.C., commemorates the sacrifice made by the 58,235 U.S. service personnel who died in the war.

# Time Line

**1954:** French are defeated at Dien Bien Phu; Vietnam is divided.

**1955:** U.S. agrees to train the South Vietnamese army; Soviet Union and China aid North Vietnam.

**1962:** U.S. military advisers in South Vietnam are increased to 12,000.

**1964:** August, USS *Maddox* is reportedly approached by North Vietnamese Navy torpedo boats in Gulf of Tonkin; Congress passes the Gulf of Tonkin Resolution.

**1965:** First U.S. combat forces arrive in Vietnam; by year's end, troops total over 200,000.

**1967:** 500,000 American troops are in Vietnam.

**1968:** January, Tet Offensive is launched; March, Lyndon B. Johnson announces that he will not seek re-election; June, Robert Kennedy is assassinated; August, riots disrupt the Democratic Convention in Chicago; November, Richard Nixon is elected President.

**1969:** Nixon begins slow withdrawal of U.S. forces; secret bombing of Cambodia begins; My Lai massacre is revealed; 250,000 protesters march in antiwar demonstration in Washington, D.C.

**1970:** U.S. ground forces enter Cambodia; antiwar protests spread across U.S.; four students are killed at Kent State University; U.S. troops in Vietnam are reduced to 280,000; December, Congress repeals the Gulf of Tonkin Resolution.

**1972:** Nixon increases bombing of North Vietnam.

**1973:** January, peace accords are signed in Paris, France; March, last U.S. ground troops leave Vietnam.

**1975:** January, North Vietnam announces an all-out offensive to seize South Vietnam; April, last U.S. citizens are evacuated from Saigon; North Vietnamese take Saigon.

# Glossary

**advisor:** someone who gives advice or guidance

**briefing:** a meeting in which information or directions are given

**communist:** person who believes in a system of social organization in which all property and goods are owned by the government and shared equally with all people

**conscientious objector:** a person who refuses to fight in the armed forces or bear arms on moral or religious grounds

**defoliation:** the use of chemicals to kill trees and plants

**flashback:** a past incident recurring vividly in the mind

**GIs:** U.S. military personnel

**guerrilla:** a person who engages in irregular warfare, especially as a member of an independent unit carrying out harrassment or acts of sabotage

**lobby:** to conduct activities aimed at influencing public officials, especially members of a legislative body

**mortar:** a short, large-caliber cannon that fires high into the air

**napalm:** a form of jellied petroleum used in incendiary bombs

**pardon (v):** to absolve from the consequences of a fault or crime

**teletype:** a device for printing messages received by telegraphic relay

# Further Reading

## BOOKS

**Levy, Debi**. *Vietnam War*. Minneapolis: Lerner Publishing Group, 2004.

**White, Ellen Emerson**. *The Journal of Patrick Seamus Flaherty: United States Marine Corps, Khe Sanh, Vietnam*. New York: Scholastic, Inc., 2002.

**Willoughby, Douglas**. *Vietnam War*. Portsmouth, NH: Heinemann Library, 2001.

**Wright, David K**. *Vietnam*. New York: Scholastic, Inc., 1989.

## WEB SITES

### The American Experience in Vietnam
www.pbs.org/wgbh/amex/vietnam
*This site provides a wealth of information on the Vietnam War.*

### Vietnam Veterans of America
www.vva.org
*The Vietnam Veterans of America is one of many organizations devoted to helping Vietnam veterans.*

### Vietnam Travel/Lonely Planet Guide
www.lonelyplanet.com/destinations/south_east_asia/vietnam
*This site provides information about the country of Vietnam, the people, culture, and more.*

# Index